18 LETTERS AT 18

VIDHI GOYAL

Copyright © Vidhi Goyal
All Rights Reserved.

ISBN 979-888591445-1

This book is dedicated to someone out there,

someone special; who is just as confused

about things as I am

Contents

Acknowledgements

To my parents and my online friends,

    thankyou for encouraging me to write this book

1. Shivani- It was a great opportunity to have been able to write a letter with you [@vaanibyshivani]
2. Mayank- When you released your book, it inspired me to write one [@healing.the.broken]
3. Tanavi- Thankyou for hyping me up <3 [@renaissance_inks]
4. Tanushree and Pragya- Thankyou for being there [@tanuuuuu_writes and @shhh.she.is.dreaming]

1. A LETTER TO THE HOME I'M LEAVING BEHIND//

""It has been 4905 days, i.e., 13 years-5months-3days since I have been living with you. Each day of my life has felt like an opportunity to grow with you! But now, I have to leave you. I often wonder that just how fast the night changes; one day I took my first step for you and now, 13 years later, I'll be taking the last step as I should leave you""

6 years later, I'm here but-
you are still there
I haven't moved on from what happened
but you're still there waiting for someone;
someone - but not me
It's been 6 years and still I am having a hard time
trying to forget the passionate love we had
but this society didn't like our love I guess
That's why,
I'm here and you're there; waiting for someone;
someone- but not me

-VIDHI

2. A LETTER TO THE HOME I'M MAKING MINE//

Leaving behind my previous lover,

I come into your arms;
they aren't as soothing as the ones before
but you're hell bent on making it somehow
''6 years later I'm trying to not fall out in love with these arms"
but it seems like these arms don't want me anymore''
I have doubts for this relationship
for even 6 years later,
I'm still stuck over the fact that I'm with you
and not with my previous love

-VIDHI

3. A LETTER TO SOMEONE I LOST A LONG TIME AGO//

We were so in love...or at least I thought;

The last time I read your letter, I got devastated.

I remember one line you mentioned, "your tears have a peculiar sweetness; that's why I love seeing you cry"

I still remember this line, and everytime it makes me remember the days when I went by crying but you couldn't do anything to make me stop crying.

Because of course you liked the sweetness of my tears!

You saw the melodious pain behind my tears and let me live in the silent chaos from being tied by a chain of miseries.

I lost you a long time ago. But it's safe to say that I don't miss you; I don't miss the album of memories we made or the overwhelming wounds you gave me.

I know that somewhere my heart might miss you; but I'm writing a new page of hope with beautiful distractions and a touch of ecstatic bliss

4. A LETTER TO JUST...SOMEONE//

I was just beginning to weave the threads of memories to avoid the midnight cacaphony while playing with my curls when the butterfingers of mine found a journal-a journal WE wrote. I did not want to but eventually I opened it.

I found a picture of us sitting under the oak tree with seashells in your hand and tangy toffees in mine. Next, I found some stained pages. In your calligraphic style you wrote me a poem titled AN ODE TO LOVE. On another stained page I wrote you a twilight tale.

I turned to the next page. It was another photograph of us- but the best one. In that moment. remembered we were having rainbow smiles on our face while we were swinging flashlights on each other. On the next page, I found a poem. I remembered!! I was standing before the mirror describing myself as the ugly face with acne all over it- but then you described me as a cute panda.

Now I started crying hard. Those tears of mine looked like dewdrops on my soul. The cacaphony had stopped but now my mind was like a plain silver screen, demanding to fulfill all those smoky desires I promised to myself, demanding to forget our first as well as our last meeting at the crossroads, demanding to move on from it -for this end will be the

beginning of something new
-VIDHI

5. A LETTER TO SOMEONE WHO PROBABLY WON'T READ THIS

""We met,we talked

Then the sun came up and reality set in"

Now I know what the reality is;

As you're not here but I am

As you are somewhere doing something you enjoy

But I'm here alone

Doing something I don't want to-

Missing you

But as I said,"the sun came up and reality set in....it was epic"

It was epic to have got to know you

It made me realise how hard I can love someone and yet not

be loved at all at the same time

\- VIDHI

6. A LETTER TO SOMEONE LIVING IN MY MIND//

I'm not feeling well

Something is going on in my mind

A voice I can hear and I cannot hear

Some screams

Internally,I am crying, screaming

But from the outside,I'm expressionless- no one can tell what's going on inside me

Hell I don't know what's going on inside my body

Feels as if my heart wants to say something; not something but a lot of things

My mind wants to explode. It just wants to get rid of the overthinking I guess.

But how

I want to cry

I am ready to cry

Hell I'm crying internally

The difference is that the tears just won't show on my face

Plus I'm wearing a mask due to this pandemic

-VIDHI

7. A LETTER TO THE PERSON WHO IS TIRED OF LIVING//

I don't even have the guts to ask you how you are doing? A person having suicidal thoughts is already dieing bit by bit everyday.

How should I start? What conversation shall I have with you? Maybe, letter was the best option I had.

You once told me how much you adore life and today you are the one telling me that life is a nightmare. You tried putting an effort to make some sense in life. I know your efforts went in vain.

Your drowned eyes with poisonous tears, stale mind with vulnerable thoughts, visible scars by the demons say a lot about the things you went through. It isn't easy to live in such terrible state.

But you know, your life doesn't consist of only you. You have family, friends, well wishers who have you in their prayers. Have you ever thought of them?

How will they live without you? What will be your best friend's reaction when they come to school and you won't be there? Also, your family can't just live looking at your photographs.

You have a significant mark in your loved ones life. Even your dog will wonder where did you suddenly disappear and that why is no one playing with him/her

Giving up on life isn't the solution. I understand you have ropes of miseries and exhaustion tied around you but a slightest effort to untie them can make a big difference

You can't just hold on to dark moments forever. There's always a ray of sunshine coming your way everyday.
Your past is just an album of censored memories;only accessible to you. Your future is a whole new album of hope and opportunities. You can make your future a new album of relishing memories. It's all within you!!

You have a universe within you. Try filling it with constellations of happiness and success. Try making it so strong that no one dares to destroy it
.

So for just once,think,think about everyone,and maybe- think about me too
-VIDHI
[A NOTE TO READERS// I WROTE THIS LETTER ALONG WITH MY ONLINE FRIEND-
@vaanibyshivani ON INSTAGRAM]

8. A LETTER TO THE SOCIETY WHO HAD EXPECTATIONS FROM ME//

*"*One day you're going to have to stop pretending everything's okay* – Elena Gilbert"*

This is a quote from one of my favourite web series, The Vampire Diaries

This quote reminds me of so many people's expectations from us

//THEY EXPECT ME TO SOCIALIZE EVEN MORE\\
She says,"You can't live your life like this,stranded alone-all by yourself,not even allowing a single soul to enter your life"
But how do I tell her that the last time I socialized with someone,I fell for them,they left me and I lost a piece of myself

//THEY EXPECT ME TO EXPRESS MY FEELINGS\\
She says,"You don't have to keep quiet all the time, everyone is

bound to have some emotions. Just let them out- maybe just talk about them"
But how do I tell her that the last time I tried expressing my feelings,someone disrespected the same feelings and that again I lost a piece of myself;this time a major one.

//THEY EXPECT ME TO HAVE FRIENDS\\
She says,"You just have to make friends,that is easy,once you make friends, everything will be easy"
But how do I tell her that the last time I had a friend,she left me....She didn't say anything-she just left me. And this time,I lost ...I lost what all was left inside me.

//EXPECTATIONS MADE ME LOSE MYSELF\\
You see people had so much expectations from me,they still have
They want me to do so many things. They want me to socialize,they want me to this,they want to do that
But how? How can I fulfill these expectations when all they do is make me lose me more and more
-VIDHI

9. A LETTER TO SOMEONE WHOM I CAN'T RESIST FALLING FOR

HOW CAN I NOT FALL FOR YOU?

As those honeyed eyes interlock with mine,
For the first time I don't think about a lonely tomorrow,
I don't think if I care about my life being sweet and sour like my food

As those caramel lips blow a smile towards me,
I feel like I'm lost in a dream
The only thought wandering my mind is to look for my lost soul amidst those pine-trees forest and give it to him

How can I not fall for him
When all he does is give me a smirk and make me ache for a wilder; moonlit moment

I never told you that but a search for foraging led me under the canopies where I carry you in my visions and wonder if change is really coming

-VIDHI

10. A LETTER TO THE PERSON WHO WANTS TO ESCAPE REALITY

POV- You are tired from being ignored

Why is it always like this? we both are here;

but it seems as if only you are visible to them: other people

can see me,but not you;and nor they who see only you

I want to scream sometimes! but I often think that whom

should I scream on?

Should i scream on you because you are their first choice?

Should i scream on myself for being ignored? Or should i

scream on them for ignoring me out?

-VIDHI

11. A LETTER TO ALL THE WHAT IF'S

To know what I can do beyond my limits yet be feared from the one immortal;

this is a letter to the undestructable- a perfect match for this society- WHAT IF'S

I started to climb the ladder to success; when a thorn named WHAT IF struck my leg

I took it off wiped the blood,knowing it would stop in a moment

As i moved further towards my destination, my leg got stuck in a stone and I fell down

the stone had the words WHAT IF engraved on them I hesitated and started moving further

After every now and then, I found you with me sometimes behind me,sometimes slapping me across the face

everytime I moved forward, you pulled me 2 steps back and shoved yourself in my face

Finally I climbed the ladder only to find another ladder with a lot more WHAT IF'S and a bit less comfort

-VIDHI

12. A LETTER TO ALL THE MAYBE'S

I heard from a friend of mine, you came into town and destroyed the WHAT IF'S

so I decided that I'll meet you not knowing that your addiction was even worse than the what if's

So one fine day I decide to go out, I wear that revealing outfit, not knowing your eyes were already on me

when suddenly my mind ponders about that creepy guy downside the road,

when suddenly my mind thinks about something crazy I decided to do that night

And I knew that you were in town

and that your eyes were on me

and my mind got hypnotised in the web of ALL THE MAYBE'S

-VIDHI

13. A LETTER TO THE BOY WHO'LL LOVE HER NEXT

To the boy who will love her next,

1. Keep assuring her- Don't let her think at any point of time that she is unworthy or does not deserves to have you. She is already fragile at this moment. You need to give her time to heal

2. See to her emotions- Look after her,care for her,make her believe that you are and will be there for her

3. Pamper her- Whenever she feels low, do not ask her why. Instead, pamper her with your love and affection. Shower her with kisses on her forehead,cuddle up with her

4. And last but not the least, do not lie to her- If you think she won't agree to a thing,do not lie. She is trying moving on from the thorns of lies forced onto her skin. So don't try to pull apart the bandage

-VIDHI

14. A LETTER TO THE GIRL WHO'LL LOVE HIM NEXT

To the girl who will love him next,

1. Make him believe he's worthy- He might think that he's not worthy of love; specially from you. But it's your duty to make him believe that he was and will always be worthy of everyone's love, including yours

2. Make sure he releases the toxic blood time to time- For the time being, his body is on antibiotics and other healing supplements. But you got to make sure that he takes a break from them once in a while so as to get rid of some of the toxic blood. let that bandage rip; but slow and steadily

3. Show him your love- Show him some love;whether he asks or not. Make some good memories with him, but at the same time make sure that you do not force him to do so. Make him a playlist, buy him chocolates and do whatever it takes for him to realize that he is loved

4. And last but not the least, do not lie to him- If you think he won't agree to a thing,do not lie. He is trying moving on from the thorns of lies forced onto his skin. So don't

try to pull apart the bandage

- VIDHI

15. A LETTER TO THE EYES WHICH SHED TEARS FOR SOMEONE ELSE

To the eyes which shed tears; but for someone else,

When I took birth; you announced my arrival by shedding some tears When I learnt to walk and fell down for the first time, you shed some tears

and my mom comforted us both - her touch convinced us both not to cry anymore

After a few years, you started shedding tears; but for someone else

At that moment, I knew I had to comfort both of us because I knew mom would scold us for crying over someone else

But how could I do it when I had no idea how to? So I let you; I let you shed tears for someone else

until I was exhausted; until you were exhausted

But now it's time, It's time for both of us to move on and stop shedding tears for someone else

-VIDHI

16. A LETTER TO THE PERSON WHO TURNED INTO A STRANGER

To the person who turned into a stranger,

I won't ask why, for I no longer have the energy to survive another heartbreak

I won't ask why, for I know that people usually find me annoying and eventually leave me

For I think that what we had, was never true

For I think how excellent you pretended to be crazy for me

Because you see, if you were actually crazy about me, You wouldn't have left me

We would be here, together

Not with us being strangers again, but this time with memories

-VIDHI

17. A LETTER TO THE VICTIMS OF ONE-SIDED LOVE

To the people dying in one sided love,

"*"सब कुछ वही है, पर कुछ कमी है, तरी आहट नही है"*"

This is all we can think of when we are dying for their love
How naive we can be for that one person that we literally can turn impossible things into a possibility,just to have a glimpse of them or maybe even talk to them!
One-sided love- this is the worst death for us hopeless romantics

We don't want to be their friends,we want to be a bit more important to them; but not too important
All we can think of is confessing our love to them 24/7 but we know we can't do that
My dear friends, I salute you for being in that one-sided thing because I know how much it hurts

"*But all we can think is of a possibility, maybe, "पहल, क्यो न मलि हम"*"

-VIDHI

18. A LETTER TO LETTERS

To letters,

"To write is human, to receive a letter: Devine!"
~Susan Lendroth

Sitting by the window side on a rainy day,
with a mug of hot coffee, laptop and listening to "love is raining" spotify playlist
I think about letters ;
How people waited for days, just to recieve a letter. Those good old days when one would just wait for a glimpse of the postman!!!!!
And as I take the first sip from my coffee, I start writing about you

a letter to letters

I asked my grandmother, "what did letters meant to you" and she replied that," your grandfather would often send me some before the marriage" and she blushed

I asked my little cousin," would you like to recieve a letter" and he replied that," Maybe Santa Claus will send me one if I behave good" and he asked for his Christmas gift

Then I asked myself,"would i send someone a letter?" and I began writing what would I write if I were to send a letter to someone

"How wonderful it is to be able to write someone a letter! To feel like conveying your thoughts to a person, to sit at your desk and pick up a pen, to put your thoughts into words like this is truly marvelous."
— Haruki Murakami, Norwegian Wood

-VIDHI

9 7 9 8 8 8 5 9 1 4 4 5 1